Ͱ

Savvy

Restaurant Reviewer

The secrets of a restaurant critic.

By Sam Worthington

Other books by the same author

(www.books.samworthington.com)

The Aquitaine Trilogy (the development of a new society after a holocaust.)
The General (The first book of The Aquitaine Trilogy)
The Constitution (The second book of The Aquitaine Trilogy)
The War (The third book of The Aquitaine Trilogy)

Hookers Hero (1970s era thriller set in London and the UK)
Kelly: the bar girl who would be president (Asia politics as they are)
A Superlative View (the world of two Labradors)

Food and travel writing
www.samworthington.com
Political Blog
www.asiabugle.com

Contents

1. What it is all about?

As a high profile restaurant reviewer of two ex-pat papers in Budapest and Warsaw, I was considered the authority on eating out. The inevitable consequence of this was that when I met somebody new - once they realised who I was as I used a *nom de plume* - they asked, "well, what is the best restaurant here?"

That may appear to be a comparatively simple call - after all we used to run a restaurant of the year competition. But in reality the answer is fraught with danger. Whatever I may think, my view is it is an opinion - a considered opinion maybe and a highly qualified opinion as well as I have dined all over the world - but it is still my view and open to challenge. Of course the secret of being a successful restaurant reviewer is to empathise with your readers. You will not last long if you say a place is good and everybody else thinks it is not.

But I would answer that question with a question, "What," I would say, "do you want?" Then I would ask "is it for a high powered business meeting? A romantic evening? A friendly meal with a friend, and if so what kind of friend? Or is for a party to have a bit of fun?" The point here is that in the restaurant business, as much as in the horse racing business, it is a very much "horses for courses." A Derby horse is not a National horse – but that does not prevent both from being excellent animals!

"THE PERFECT LIGHT SNACK"

Another issue that will invariable come up is price. That can be divisive as well because we all eat different things, drink different amounts and have different ideas about what is expensive and what is not. A meal in London's West End is almost certainly going to be more expensive than a similar meal in, say, rural Wales. Just as relevant is what a meal constitutes: my idea of the perfect light snack for lunch is a lobster and a bottle of Gewürztraminer and I would expect to pay lot more for that than a plate of pasta and a small carafe of house wine - which is not really lunch at all!

But if somebody said, "did you have a good lunch and how much was it?" To answer "yes" and quote the price of my lunch tells them nothing, without a description of the meal. Similarly if I go out to dinner with a friend, and drink three bottles of wine, the price will be great deal more than for a more modest gathering of water drinkers. So either the meal has to be described in detail along with the price, or given a general description suggesting the price was in line with what would be expected in that kind of establishment.

The latter method is preferable when writing on the internet, as so often those articles stay around for years and five years later what you paid is probably out of date. I often caused a certain amount of derision when dining - particularly with my friend Lord Toad - by adding comments like 'after three bottles of half decent wine and few calavas (calvados) the bill was a modest ....' Of course it is all grist to the reviewer's mill, and reputation!

Humour is a double edged sword - get it right and it enhances the review but all too often a joke is not appreciated by every reader - particularly as humour does not travel well across cultures. The same goes for sarcasm and facetious comments: they need to work and using them badly can make the writer look the fool, not the intended target.

On this point recently I had an interesting discussion with an American who had run a successful pub in LA. "What," he asked me, "is the vital ingredient of a good English pub?"

'There are not many left in the UK,' I thought, and then explained a few things about communities and who you have, and who you don't have, in the bar. Next I said, "If you walk into good old fashioned boozer you are likely to be told to bugger off."

The American looked puzzled.

"Or you could be the rear end of a human," I replied to his unanswered question, adding a little humour hoping he would get the point. As it dawned on him what I meant I added, "Of course such a greeting in the U S of A may get you shot."

"Ah," he said, "anything as long as you are recognised." Bingo! To be called a rude name meant you were 'in.'

Needless to say what I am getting at is a new reviewer needs to think about how they will write their reviews. Will they be easy-to-read reviews gently poking the restaurant with some light hearted observations which try to give an overall impression of what the place is like? Or will they be meticulous in detail allowing the reader to build up a specific image of the place?

I am not a writing coach - far from it. However what I do know is you need to be readable - that means your readers must want to read your prose and find it easy to do so. Consequently your personality needs to come across.

Ostensibly you need to become an extrovert who knows and loves their subject. Realistically, you need to know what good food is, but not a great deal about the technicalities as the internet now provides much information - both good and bad - and a reviewer no longer needs to live with a Larousse Gastronomique. (I am on my third copy.)

But beware of believing everything the web tells you. If I need to look things up I take two or three answers, or more

9

if there is a discrepancy between them, before I will settle on what looks right. I normally have a good idea of the answer so I am checking, more than getting new knowledge. If you really do not know, the best advice is avoid, and work round, the issue lest you make a fool of yourself!

One other tip: MS word has a spell checker that tends to be American and not English – you can adjust it to English UK and do if that is your language. However another useful tool is the right click on a word for synonyms – as every writer knows looking for different ways to say the same thing is part of the art and I write with a thesaurus by my side – I still have it after 30+ years.

MS word can often be stupid – well it would be, wouldn't it – when it comes to spelling. And my dyslexia can completely fool it. However Google search is much cleverer. Type a badly spelt word into Google and invariably you get the right answer. You can also check word meanings and use online thesauruses. So the web can be truly the author's friend – you just need to know how to harness it for good, but beware of false counsel.

The main thing your reviews need is a point of view. Use strong adjectives and don't be afraid of the word 'foul' -

foul fowl will make most at least smile except, of course, the restaurateur and the unfortunate fowl who died in vain - or was it from old age?

And that brings me to the point of criticism - it is a nasty reality of life that bad news sells and good news does not. It is the aeroplane thing - the news is not that there were a million successful take offs and landings last week: it is that there was one unsuccessful one. Unfortunately that means bad restaurant reviews are more popular than good ones and there are well known reviewers who specialise in knocking any restaurant they visit. It might make them more readable but it does not provide credibility - all bad is as worthless as all good. The answer is that there are usually some good points, but few restaurants are perfect. Tough but fair is not a bad reputation to aim for.

There is another issue about criticism: have a thought for the restaurateur who has often put his/her soul and life's savings into the project. You can do him/her a great deal of damage and there are few restaurants that do not have some redeeming features.

Offhand I can only think of two in the many years I have been writing reviews that I really thought were so bad they deserved to be closed down. In those cases everything was wrong. But just as importantly, I saw no positive signs - the food was bad and it was clear nobody understood food and nobody cared enough even if they did.

In such cases a reviewer may feel they have a duty to the paying public, to get the place shut down. However the reality is most people are trying hard, even if they are getting it all wrong, and at least deserve plaudits be it only for effort. I can honestly say in my time I have both made and broken a restaurant or two, but overall I like to think I provided fair judgement that should have helped the owners improve their operation.

And another point well worth making is that your views are both subjective in terms of the timing of your visits, and to your own personal foibles. Inevitably, too, other visitors may arrive on a different day and have alternative perspectives. However your followers will be people who are of similar mind to yourself.

I will briefly mention smoking as these days in Europe the PC non smokers have had their way and smoking is *verboten* inside almost all restaurants and bars. But sometimes a provision is made for those 'who must.' Outside Europe the

PC mafia have not yet fully had their way so the issue maybe worth mentioning in a review if the local norm does not apply.

So having decided what kind of reviewer you want to be and established your style of review, all that remains is to go and do it.

I would recommend one piece of kit - a camera. If you want pictures to illustrate your article it is a good idea to make certain you know how to take food pictures: it is not easy particularly as the lighting will usually be wrong, so a little practice will help.

A camera is also good as a note taker, not just of the food itself so you can see exactly what you ate, but also for recording details of the menu and wine list. Smart phone cameras have come a long way and will certainly do for notes, and probably for internet articles. However a better camera will be needed for print illustration. How much better will depend on the quality of the publication. Of course for truly professional magazines, a professional photographer will go round after you and get the shots required.

The final requirement is a notebook and pen. Never rely solely upon memory - and sometimes thoughts and small incidents, that will add important colour to the review, occur during the meal and maybe forgotten if not recorded. Some people these days may prefer to make notes using a smartphone or tablet device, but this may look pretentious and disruptive in the intimate ambience of a restaurant. Sometimes, 'simple' works best.

Many of my reviews are done on my own. I always joke that I enjoy dining alone because I can have a more interesting conversation. However I freely admit the more the merrier when reviewing is appropriate, as a true cross section of the menu can then be sampled.

However one point worth noting – small restaurants in particular are not geared up for large groups wandering in unannounced. So if over four in a small place, or six plus in larger restaurant, book – it is unfair to do otherwise and expect the same standard as for two. I know I have been in the kitchen when that surprise party arrives and thus I know all about trying to get out ten different starters and ten different mains with the aid of a grumpy kitchen porter – washer-up to you and me. If you must be an unannounced large party at least do the chef a favour and try eating the same things!

It is always said, at the head of my articles, that 'Sam Worthington pays his own way and writes what he thinks.' As a reviewer, as far as possible, I am anonymous – I tried to stop my picture being published and it certainly does not head up my articles. In my opinion that is the only way it can be.

Needless to say some restaurateurs do know me; this I know when visiting their places, and I have to look at more than my own plate. In any event I normally remain incognito throughout the visit. Sometimes at the end I will introduce myself - if I have a few questions to ask –more for curiosity's sake than anything else. However by then I have recognised, in my mind, the competence of the establishment.

One thing I never do is take money, or free meals, for writing a review. Those that do are not restaurant reviewers but writers of fluff, or maybe in the modern idiom they are 'reputation managers.' You will probably still benefit from reading this book, but it is not aimed at you!

2. The first impression

This section is very much about getting into the review and can be as long or as short as you think is needed - it introduces the place.

To start with it is not a bad idea to let your readers know why you choose this particular restaurant ... "a friend mentioned," or "a reader was good enough to suggest," "I was walking past and the goose on the menu caught my eye," or something similar, or "in France I often pick a restaurant for lunch because it has a full car park."

Then having explained why you picked the place you need to write what you think is necessary to give a feel for it. "I booked a table and was told there were two sittings" tells your readers it is a busy restaurant and they might be hassled out if on the first sitting.

Efficiency at all levels is a good sign, though of course calling in the middle of a busy service period is a not a good time in a small restaurant without a full time receptionist. In a big one, however, it is reasonable to expect an efficient booking process. Certainly losing a booking because it has not been written down is big minus - more so if booking way in advance is needed.

How to find the place can also be important if it is not easy: a general description of the location always helps. That is particularly relevant if the place is hidden away in the boondocks, or down an obscure urban side street. Sometimes when *you* know exactly where a place is, it can seem superfluous to go into details of how to find it. Put yourself in your reader's shoes and imagine that you have no knowledge of the area – then how easy is it?

The outside and then walking through the door are the moments when your first views are formed. If the building looks tidy, and the outside is inviting, that is good. In a rural setting the external appearance is often more important than in a city. However if you are trundling around looking for a meal with someone else, how often do you say, "that place looks good!" And because of that appearance you may walk past another place to look at the menu, or peek inside – appearance always counts as any self respecting *gourmet* will tell you

Then the critical moment: walking through the door. That first sensation can be critical - it maybe elegance, it may be that the place is buzzing, it may be the prompt, warm, genuine reception, or it may be something totally different. The smell can be very significant; a nasty smell will ruin any perception. The most common one is the pervasion of cooking oil which could be old oil that should have been changed, or that there is no extraction system in the kitchen. Either way it is not a good smell to walk into.

On the other hand good food smells are just what you want ... or flowers, especially if there is a good display ... or even furniture polish. A most memorable smell to me was a restaurant in Budapest with only one real menu item: roast pig hocks. It had all these spits gently turning with hocks on them

- the place smelt of gentle roasting pork. Writing this, years later, I can still smell them and my mouth is watering. Not so good if your idea of food is a well-washed dandelion leaf but to any meat eater.....!

How you get treated as you arrive is incredible important. If you are quickly greeted - even if not dealt with - but if a busy person smiles and says "one minute please," you feel reassured. Conversely, even if they're busy, if everybody is scampering about and you are ignored you will quickly take offence.

A walk-in (without a prior reservation) cannot complain if they are greeted and then asked to wait a moment whilst a table is sorted. To an extent the same applies if there is a booking and the place is busy. Of course you may be directed to a bar and looked after there. There is no fixed format: everywhere is different. But the issue is simple. Are you looked after and made to feel welcome?

Exactly what constitutes a good welcome is up the establishment itself, as well as the guest's perception. On that note any restaurateur will tell stories of unreasonable and selfish demands. As a reviewer, it is your job to be Ms or Mr Average. You may have high standards, but at the same time you acknowledge that staff members only have two hands and that good food takes time to prepare and deliver.

It has been said that the first impression is the most important in almost all relationships and it is certainly so in a restaurant. If a few minutes after you have arrived you are sitting, feeling relaxed and cared for, then you feel welcome and you will be more tolerant of everything else that follows.

Needless to say vice versa is just as true. Being waved to a table in a busy bistro is fine, whereas in a place providing fine dining more attention is expected. And we all have our own ideas of what is a good setting and what is not. As a reviewer you need to set the scene and few words will normally suffice.

3. The menu and wine list

You have been greeted and seated so the first thing you need - after a drink maybe - is the menu. You could even argue that getting the menu and wine list is part of the greeting process; it certainly is in bistros and fast food joints. The wine list is particularly important to people who, like me, may want to order a bottle of white wine as an *apéritif*, which can then usually stretch over the opening courses.

Although most restaurants understand that their main business is selling food, believe you me I have been to a few that have other aspirations. It is usually feeding the ego of the proprietor, or sometimes it is simply feeding the staff for doing as little as possible. Inevitably they only last as long as the owner's pockets are deep, and at times even that is too long! But assuming the place you are in is doing what its name suggests, then getting a list of their products to you ASAP should be an essential.

The internet can save the reviewer much work as most restaurants have a website with the menu and wine list on it. Directing your readers to that site is good because it will keep them up to date with both changes in the menus and prices.

In many ways the menu is the most important part of the business and for reviewers, giving a good feel of the menu is essential. By feel I mean not just the type of food, but also the depth and range of the offerings. I usually say something like "the mains included six meats options, three fish as well a statutory veggie offering."

Of course you need to describe the type of food if it is not a restaurant with a specific ethnicity. Very often the menu will have a blurb saying a little about the background of the owner and thus the source of the recipes - Italians seem to be particularly keen on telling everybody where they came from and singing the praises of that region.

Since the ethnicity of the place is the most important menu issue for most people, inevitably ethnic restaurants of the same ilk tend to have similar menus. Thus it is up the reviewer to look for the menu items that are not the norm. In a way the restaurants of a country are ethnic too – be it of that country or region. So the menu needs summing up in a few concise words and then a few different, or exceptional dishes, can be explained.

In this book I am doing the review in clear layers. However when you are writing your reviews, the layers may well be intermingled – e.g. with menu description followed by what actually arrived, all in the same sentence. That's fine in an actual review.

It is not unusual for restaurants to have two, three or more menus. In France they are keen on their menus and these are normally much cheaper than going *à la carte*. As a reviewer, quantifying the different menus is vital – how much detail is up to you.

I am sucker for a menu *dégustation* – they vary but in general they are a tasting type menu and should display the best cooking the kitchen can provide. On top of that *dégustation* menus are normally 4 to 6 courses and expensive. So whilst they may show the abilities of the establishment's kitchen they may not provide particularly useful information for a reader who does not want to splash out.

The other problem I have found in France, in particular, is that *dégustation* menus all too often feature the same items – *foie gras* and pigeon seem to be the current 21st century favourites.

The menu at the other end of the scale – the daily menu - is normally a good option for a review, albeit a little boring.

Daily menus, in decent restaurants, on the whole represent value as well as good simple cooking. Regional menus are often interesting with different dishes. However it is your review and you decide what you want to review and that may well be decided by budget. What is needed is a description of the menu options and selected dishes from them; then what the reviewer has decided to eat and why.

Assuming the reviewer is not alone then it is important that every diner concerned selects differently, and to that end the reviewer's own selection is best made after the his/her companions have decided. Variety is the spice of a review.

The wine list is usually little more than a complementary offering of a simple range of different wine types by country, region, colour, grape, year and price. I am by no means an expert on wine, but I suppose I know my way round a wine list - and so I should … I have had enough practice.

But wine as I am sure you are aware is a highly specialised subject that is best left to the experts. It is also an important part of the meal so it deserves significant mention by outlining the choices available and I usually mention price as well. I know this goes against my comments on the meal price but wine is a peculiar item, in that there is little consistency in pricing. Some restaurants – particularly outside Europe – seem to think if a person is dumb enough to drink wine they deserve to be ripped off.

However even within Europe there are very different ways of applying the margin to wine. The house wine is important: there is a feeling that the house wine should represent the establishment as much as the food. My view is it should certainly be drinkable – yet I have had some house wines that would not have disgraced fish and chips – assuming Sarson's and chips takes your fancy.

That takes me back to those awful days of the seventies when 'dry white wine' was all the rage – the drier the better - how people drank it I have no idea!

But fortunately we have moved on and there is massive range of wines available to most restaurants. The reviewer should précis the list so the reader has some idea of their options – I usually mention the house, or least expensive wine, as well as a couple from the top end.

Of course there are restaurants with staggering wine lists usually featuring the wines of a region. Many restaurants in the Bordeaux region of France have a huge and comprehensive list of local wines which, in their case, means some of the finest vineyards in the world.

Some of the older wines need decanting and really cannot be drunk at short notice. I love those lists and I sit a drool over one when I see it. The listings are normally in a weighty leather bound folder – I always then feel a little embarrassed when I order something not that special! But I enjoy the read - gasping at Cheval Blancs and Château Margaux made when I was in short trousers. Well worth literalising over when writing the review.

At this stage I have not mentioned dessert wines and ports, etcetera, which I will deal with at the appropriate time – that is of course unless you want a bottle decanted for later!

4. Foreplay

Now you know what you want to order, all you need is somebody to convey that information to the kitchen: you need an order taker. And there is nothing more frustrating that sitting around waving a menu and nothing happens. In practice, most restaurants know that getting your order is important: once they have got that, you are committed.

Another annoying trait is when they suddenly announce your choice is not to be had. As a restaurateur I do not mind if some dishes are not available; food needs to be fresh and items do run out. However I want to be told that *before* I look at the menu, not after I have decided what I want.

It is also worth checking whether the person taking the order understands the menu. Ask a few questions even if you do not need to – just to check their knowledge. It is not a bad idea to ask for recommendations and the answer is not *'it's all good...'* that is a cop out.

The wine list is often fun, unless there is a *sommelier* in which case it is better to shut up and not display your ignorance. However asking for wine recommendations from most servers is more likely to confuse than to inform.

Having ordered it is time to sit back, relax and study the surroundings. I find I can learn a great deal about a place by simple watching it operate. Of course having been a restaurateur myself I have the experience, and know what to look for when watching other tables, and the food being served. The reaction of the fellow diners is always a good indication of how the place works.

Observe if people are waiting for service. Are they all happy and enjoying themselves? Do the staff look like they know what they are doing? Is there a supervisor keeping an eye on what is happening? How are new arrivals treated? The review is about your food and your experience. However watching the whole production is revealing and thus helpful.

The décor has been covered above, but what about table settings? Nice starched table napkins with a button hole in the corner ... a fad of mine so we chaps can attach the napkin to the shirt, otherwise the damn things keep slipping down to around one's ankles where they are of little use. And when that happens does a waiter rush over with a crisp new one?

Are there good wine glasses and a decent cruet set? I am not very keen on chefs who think they know how to season my food and thus hide the salt and pepper. Having said that I always taste before seasoning; to do otherwise is presumptuous.

How the service proceeds will depend upon the type of establishment. In a busy bistro hopefully somebody dumps a bottle of wine on the table with glasses and maybe a carafe of water. But in a more upmarket environment how the wine and water arrive, and are served, is important.

White wine should be chilled and in an ice bucket.

Red wine should be at room temperature – by room temperature it means a room in temperate northern Europe. In the tropics it needs to refrigerated and then allowed to come out in the glass – and it does that remarkable quickly. Conversely red wine at tropical room temperature would be called mulled wine in a ski resort!

The recommended procedure is that the diner is shown the bottle, it is opened and then a taster measure is offered. In more pretentious places a sommelier may sniff the cork, and check the wine themselves. I must admit I get rather bored with the whole procedure. Wine is sometimes off, particularly in the tropics because getting good wine to the market without boiling it a couple of times (in a container on the Indian Ocean) is tricky.

If the restaurateur has been buying young wine (under 10 years old) in Europe, it is exceedingly unlikely to be bad. And corked wine – which is when the cork fails so the wine oxidises – is obvious by look and by smell. A piece of cork floating in a glass does not suggest that the wine is corked.

What really gets my goat is the confiscation of my wine. The waiter pours about half a glass and then disappears with the bottle. No sooner have I taken a decent slurp, the glass is empty and the waiter missing, probably off confiscating elsewhere. In any event despite all the usual signals, short of sending up a flare, the wine bottle does not reappear. The server is either too busy elsewhere, or texting, or simply cannot be bothered.

At that point I have been known to de-confiscate my wine much to the *chagrin* of the maitre d' who usually rushes to the table to try and re-confiscate it. Don't take my word for it - try it for yourself!

In Thailand, wine is ludicrously expensive because of excise duty and thus even the cheapest bottle of wine in a restaurant equals a week's wages for the luckless serving staff. Consequently they seem to think it must be an ornament, not something to be consumed. They rather assume that, like the images of Buddha they keep everywhere, the customer will take it home and worship it. So, getting it opened becomes a problem – even they realise once the bottle is empty it is worthless and is certainly not worth petitioning for a favour!

W C Fields is quoted as saying words to the effect that water was simply something fish fornicated in, and I am sure he would be aghast at the absurdity of today's water menus.

For crying out loud water is water! I suppose I will grant 3 versions in a restaurant. Tap, be it from a water cooler, or mineral, is bottled water (imported from somewhere further afield than the nearest water works) with or without fizz. If some ostentatious waiter offers me a 'water menu' I reflect back to W C and say 'brown trout water please." If any of them has the wit to offer Highland Spring I suppose I would have to accept it!

Another item that causes a problem, and should not, is bread.

In less expensive places I understand the bread arriving with the starter, although in France they will always put a basket of bread on the table almost as soon as you sit down. But France has had a kind of thing about bread ever since the suggestion that *they should eat cake* instead led to the removal of the heads off all the best restaurant customers. However in smart restaurants, in countries where there was never a suggestion cake would do, bread has assumed a complication it never should have.

I remember many moons ago a long correspondence in The Caterer (The UK's premier catering magazine) among the great and good of the restaurant business in the UK about when bread should be removed from the table. That was long before the era of celebrity chefs speaking estuary English.

For some reason, some thought bread should be removed after the first course; others did not. For a reviewer, though, the presence of bread, its quality and maybe quantity are of interest and may well be worth commenting on.

So now all that is needed is some food and the *amuses bouches* arrive. Sometimes this is called the tasting spoon and that is all it is: a spoonful of food. Personally I would rather have a decent Sauvignon Blanc, or a wine from the slopes of the Vosges Mountains, do the amusing of my mouth. Thus this is not something I am particularly keen on: it is a bit like just after the start of the foreplay, being sent to have a shower.

And then you are expected to sit and wait for your food! But never mind, the shower is over – the food is on the way…

5.Food: the main event

Food, glorious food – now the whole *raison d'être* for the meal has started to arrive – or has it?

It is interesting that this is a book about restaurant reviews, yet we are now on chapter five and have only just arrived at food.

What is the main reason people go to restaurants? Food, of course, you say. The food is important; the food is the reason as in 'shall we go for a meal.' But is the food *really* the main reason? In some cases it is: but if a person simply requires sustenance, surely a sandwich would be just as good and cheaper, or, dare the thought cross my mind, why not get a burger? They are not as foul as is made out. Or a kebab. Or even a piece of flat bread with tomato sauce and other toppings on it (colloquially called a pizza).

The reality is most people go to a restaurant not for the food, but for the event. They go to socialise, they go for a business meeting, they go to be romantic, they may go to get out of the house, and they may simply want to get away from the other half's cooking. Rationally, restaurant meals are seldom about food only – they are about the event.

In this era of the 'celebrity chef,' do those who want to pay fortunes to use those chefs' establishments really go just for the victuals? Or is it to see and be seen? Or maybe it is to see the mortal whose name it was that enticed them there? Or maybe it is simply to have a night out they can talk about?

Even I, who often dine alone and enjoy it, do not go to a restaurant primarily for the food. I can, if I get off my butt, produce better food myself.

Over the many years I have been on this planet I have dined in thousands of restaurants. How many meals do I remember for the food and not the company, or the place? I am not certain; but not many. For sure I have had some marvellous meals which were truly magnificent and when that happens I go home thinking how lucky I have been. But in truth most meals, in terms of food, I forget within weeks. However I do not forget the company, or the surroundings.

So you think I am talking baloney – so be it – but think about it. A restaurant reviewer at least needs to know **why** people really go to a restaurant.

My argument about the reason for a restaurant visit may, or may not, be right, but all the same the food has to be good – or more specifically it has to be up to expectations.

Some high end restaurants' sole purpose in life is to provide truly outstanding dishes and that is what they expect to be judged on. Nevertheless they would freely admit that the surroundings and service need to be perfect: if not, why not simply serve the food that has been hours in preparation, in a canteen?

By the same token some of the best simple food in France is served in *Routiers* – a network of canteen style restaurants aimed at drivers. I always stop at one if I see one at lunch time. For what it is, the food is great, but it is not five star cooking. So the food standard has to match, or be better than, the perception of what the restaurant offers.

Most dishes will be known to your readers. As a restaurateur back in the late 1970s I found that customers were considerably less educated in culinary terms, and we often had trouble with generic dishes – *Bœuf Bourguignon, Coq au Vin* and even Cottage Pie as opposed to Shepherd's Pie.

That meant if they had a *Bœuf Bourguignon* in a specific restaurant they then thought that is how it should be, so any variant of how they 'knew it' was not, in their mind, as described. They did not comprehend that any oven cooked dish that included beef and red wine could be fairly called *bœuf Bourguignon*. That led to all kinds of problems in restaurants, but I like to think restaurant users now understand that most dishes are generic in nature: and thus are as the chef decides how those will be cooked and presented.

George Lang – a well known Hungarian restaurant entrepreneur who made his name in New York – used to say to me, "there is no such thing as an original recipe … only bad research." I am not sure he was right, but that was before the fusion of Asian and European food.

The point is, the reviewer may assume general food terminology is universally understood. But is it? Here is how I think food could be described in basic terms…

'A piece of meat 7 inches by 5 inches and about ½ inch think from the arse end of a cow' is a rump steak and that is what it should be called.'

So when considering something a bit more elaborate, to say that 'I had a very good course pork terrine with strong hint of garlic served with crusty French bread,' is more than an adequate description…

The first impression of a dish is the sight of it, and if it looks good the receiver will assume it is good. Of course if it is then found to be tough, under or over cooked, it tastes wrong or bad, it's too small a portion or simply not as described in the menu, then it is not right.

The point is that food descriptions need to be accurate; and as such, whatever was eaten by the attendees of the meal can usually be described succinctly with the minimum of words. The main thing the reader needs to know is: is the food up to the standard expected?

Sometimes the food is unusual and needs a greater description than a generic meal may demand. Excellent! Roll out descriptive words and where required, use superlatives and let the prose flow.

I have mentioned that destroying businesses is not really a reviewer's job.

However equally, it is not the reviewer's job to paper over the cracks. If something is wrong it needs to be pointed out. But it does not require a full song and dance act to do so. 'The green beans were cooked *al dente* as they should have been; pity the carrots were not the same' ... explains what was wrong in gentle way which hopefully the restaurant will pick up on. And also it proves you were paying attention.

So a few brief words about each dish will suffice. That is, as long as there is enough description for the readers to understand the style and standard of the food. By that I mean 'man-sized portions of well-cooked food' leaves an impression, as does 'well-presented and crafted dishes.' It is your review and your writing style, so decide how you want to present the food and providing the reader understands and enjoys reading it, that is all that matters.

To that end, notes are essential and photos can really help. Just a word of warning on taking photos. Most restaurants do not mind the odd swift discreet shot but other customers resent constant flashes. It is difficult to take pictures without using a flash (although many modern smart phones and digital cameras can take quite decent pictures in very low light without flash – see below.)

Nonetheless flash pictures immediately draw attention to you. Some restaurants get very sniffy if photos are taken without first asking – I have always found once asked they have no problem. I say I dine round the world and like to keep a photo record of my more memorable meals – a little bullshit smoothes the way nicely.

A serious reviewer might consider investing in a higher end digital (pocket) camera that takes a good image even in very low light, so obviating the need for any flash at all. These may not work for publishing as the results can be too pixel-ridden but they are good for notes and capturing the menu.

And such a camera will be good for food photos if used properly on the right settings.

Now for a pud!

6. Sugar and spice

I t is time for the dessert, or whatever you have
after the main courses. No – you are not slimming;
you have no health problems; you are a restaurant

reviewer and you will eat – not just red meat, fat meat, bad cholesterol, but also sugar and more fats. If you see a thin restaurant reviewer they are a fraud: or not doing much reviewing. We restaurant reviewers must regularly put our bodies on the line for our readers.

What comes next will depend upon where you are in the world. We Brits like desserts then cheese; the French want cheese before the dessert and the Italians often have cheese as a starter. As I am a Brit I want my pud next.

Desserts come in many forms from heavy traditional British puddings to lighter, simpler soufflés and mousses with all kind of tarts, crèpes, flans, trifles, custards, cakes, bombes and sundaes in between. A good plum duff may have been the dessert of choice when men were men and they toiled all day at hard physical labour but these days once a year is enough for most of us – as long as there are lashings of brandy butter!

Zuppa Inglese is a favourite of mine – an Italian version of an English trifle – at its best, soup indeed. Unfortunately the art of the dessert maker has been sidelined in many modern restaurants where puds get a token look-in with the odd 'bought in' item. But sometimes the dessert course is the one that really matters.

One Sunday I was at a loose end for a decent Sunday lunch in Montauban in central France and finally I stumbled upon *La Cuisine d'Alain*. I was told I must have the menu of the day which was acceptable rather than exciting but I had to order at the beginning. I ordered a main and starter and then said I would have cheese and the waitress said, "and dessert?" I hesitated. She appeared aghast and looked across the room. It was then I saw the dessert chariots. This is what I wrote:

"I watched the dessert chariots (note the plural) being wheeled around and the loving way in which the head waiter prepared the desserts with dribbling of this and that *coulis*, then finished the pattern off with a knife. The *foie gras* had been good and nicely cooked, the little steak had been excellent served with the interesting addition of a small tortilla type pancake, the cheese board had been massive and the cheeses were in great condition … but the whole meal was about the desserts! Not only was the dessert offering lovingly presented with virtually every type of dessert imaginable, but then in addition each helping was three desserts on the gloriously decorated plate. Before the chariot arrived a couple of taster style desserts including an éclair were presented: just to get you in the mood so to speak. I know places where those tasters would have been the dessert."

So some places take their desserts very seriously and most top restaurants have a few desserts that they make look good with spun sugar and different *coulis*. Then top hotels always have a big pastry department and thus the staff have the time and incentive to make exceptional desserts.

We reviewers have a duty to encourage the art of the pud – we can't let the PC brigade win another battle! So eat desserts we must, and then rave about them – providing of course that they are good.

Cheese is one of the great foods of Europe. We all know of Camembert, Brie, Stilton and Cheddar – and so we should; all great cheese genres. But even they have been messed around by those who insist everything should be pasteurised lest we get a nasty buggy-wuggy in our tum-tums.

Nonetheless there so many other great cheeses from Wensleydale to Mont D'Or … so there is no excuse for a bad cheese board. Except the saddest issue of all: cheese boards don't sell any more.

Gone are the days when the cheese trolley, burdened by the weight of the finest curds, turned into a staggering variety of shapes and tastes arrived at your dining table.

Far too many of the best establishments no longer even have a cheese board. Particularly in the UK and North America, an order for post-dinner cheese is filled by a plate bearing offerings of refrigerated plasticized product which insults the name of the cheeses concerned. What a terrible shame.

Inevitably, both desserts and cheese may benefit from the appropriate wine to accompany them.

It is no coincidence that the wine that is usually the most expensive *en primeur* is a dessert wine from Sauternes – but as a reviewer you are unlikely to be drinking *Château d'Yquem* although it is a good wine to comment on if it pops up on a menu.

Most decent restaurants feature a few dessert wines although the appellation is often Italian. My years in Hungary meant I drank *Tokaji* (Tokay) when it was the right price. It was still the wine of Kings – it needs at least 4 *Puttonyos*, or to be the nectar called *Eszencia*. If seen on a menu, well worth a mention.

Of course cheese deserves that other great wine – Port, or if you want something a little lighter, Madeira. Both are fortified, usually sweetish-peppery-red wines.

These days vintage port is seldom available except by the bottle and vintage port less than twenty years old is still adolescent. This vintage port worth drinking is usually nearer 50 years old and not only requires a serious investment in the worship of Bacchus, but also needs decanting at least 6 hours before drinking.

Just occasionally a restaurant will have a decanted carafe of a decent vintage port – not only worth tasting but also worth mentioning.

The usual ports on offer are Ruby, Tawny and late bottled vintage (LBV). LBV is acceptable and will improve the cheese especially if it is Stilton.

Please note: pouring port into a Stilton round just ruins both.

As a reviewer, you would do well to describe a decent list of ports – they are well worth writing about, as is the off-chance of meeting a genuine vintage Madeira. I knew of one place just outside Warminster where they had an impressive list of Madeiras. Many moons ago I started a birthday there with a lunch – not sure where it ended!

After the feasting comes the drinking and not just fortified wines but brandies and liqueurs.

Occasionally I have come across restaurants with a vast range of vintage Cognacs and even Armagnacs. But most places have a VSOP (Very Special Old Pale) at best. If you do come across a vintage cognac, or similar, remember that spirits, unlike ports and wines, mature in the cask not the bottle. Thus a 1950 Cognac bottled in 1970 is a twenty years old Cognac, whereas the same Cognac bottled in 2010 is a sixty year old, even if both are drunk now – a few years later.

Vintage brandies are not so usual, but the so-called 'stickies' are. Baileys, Tia Maria, Amaretto, Crème de Menthe to name a few – some liqueurs come from wonderful old recipes such as Benedictine, Grand Marnier and even Unicum (Hungarian). As a reviewer, you'll find that the drinking is optional but it is worth mentioning if there are interesting offerings. For me I will just have a Calva (Calvados – Apple brandy form Normandy).

There is one final course that I have not mentioned and it is almost extinct: the savoury.

After a large meal in days gone by, after much carousing and entertainment (usually dancing), a small dish was offered to sustain the revellers on their carriage ride home.

Most savouries suggest they are something that they are not. Scotch Woodcock is not a long billed wading bird but anchovies on toast with scrambled eggs, Welsh Rarebit is not an animal from the Lagomorpha family but cheese on toast; and Angels and Devils on Horseback are not the cast of the *Folies Bergères* pursued by cast of a pornographic production house, but are respectively oysters and prunes wrapped in bacon.

There is suggestion, online, that savouries are served after the dessert course in modern cuisine; I prefer the concept of after the ball is over.

So that is it: the reviewer is fed and watered. Now all you have to do is get the bill.

7. Carriages and writing

Getting the bill is important, but needless to say not painless – unless you have a sponsor. There is nothing worse than sitting around waving at the staff because you want to go home, and getting no reaction. So the speed of the arrival, the accuracy and clarity of the bill are important. In Europe credit and debit cards are the norm so there is no need to dwell on them unless for some reason they are not accepted. In certain countries it maybe the other way round – as it is in Asia where I live - so how you pay maybe of interest.

What is always of importance is the service charge. I know how much of a contentious issue that can be from the other side – when I worked as front of house staff I thought what I received I should keep … as a chef I thought I should get a share … as a manager whatever I did was wrong.

I like a *tronc* system where the weekly tips are shared equally among the staff on the basis of shifts worked. However that is not the reviewer's concern unless the system creates a problem. If in doubt I always ask if a service charge is included – assuming it is not, I add about 10% - 'about' because I will round it up or down depending upon what I thought of the food and service.

The answer I hate is – 'there is (a service charge) but we don't get it.' My answer is 'talk to your manager.' In Asia they love to say 'up to you,' which means I would like a good tip (even if it is already included).

It is not a bad idea to let readers know what you did as far as tips were concerned as a guide for them when they visit the place. Or to give some maxim … because the service charge is often as much a problem for the customers as it is for the servers.

Once the bill is paid it is time to go home – that is unless you suddenly fancy a roadie and want to see what happens when you ask for one. But eventually the door out opens. Does somebody call a taxi for you if you ask? Have they lost your hat or brolly and, if it is precipitating, does someone hold an umbrella as you walk to your carriage? All nice little final touches.

One point in this sad PC world: do not make jokes about drinking and driving – I did that once and the paper received a pile of letters to the editor – something they normally liked. But not this time as they were all about responsible journalism – the joke had backfired on me.

Now all you have to do is write it up.

On the way home it is time to reflect on the experience. What are the thoughts? An enjoyable, memorable meal? Or 'well yeah it was ok' … or 'that was a waste of money!'.

I never write a place up immediately afterwards, mainly because I have enough trouble getting my fingers to co-ordinate with the keyboard without the interference of the demon drink. But assuming I have the correct notes and photos, a few days should not affect my memory – in fact it may allow a little reflection that will improve the final story. On the other hand it is not a good idea to leave it too long – because by then things are forgotten.

I like to write my article and then leave it for a day before re-reading and editing it. So don't be in too much of a rush to publish – a little extra reflection on your essay will probably make the prose better.

The required length of a review will depend upon where it is to be published. In my prime I wrote for magazines and weekly papers which provided me with a target length of 800 – 1000 words. These days MS word helps as it provides an instant word count at the bottom of a document. However it does not really matter how long the article is – even a single sentence can cover both the food and what to expect from the place. Examples are – 'fun place with just about tolerable TexMex food in lively surroundings;' or 'high standard of cooking served in elegant, if slightly stuffy, backdrop;' or 'archetypical Italian decor with a good value menu serving acceptable food.'

In all cases the description of the environment is as important as the food. When I am asked to write 50 word descriptions for magazines and travel books and I find those remarkably hard work – trying to get nuances of a restaurant in few words as well as summing up the food is not easy.

For guide books and similar there may be a need for rankings. A scoring system should thus be developed. It should be easy enough to put a form on a smartphone, if not keep a hard copy and score each category from greeting, to decor, to loos, to service, to menu etc. Include and give more or fewer points for whatever you, and/or the editor of the publication, think is important. The most important rule of scoring is to be very (very) tough. That is because whatever happens somewhere else will be better - so starting off with 95% leaves you nowhere to go. If the best is 80% that is good – then if you want to you can always apply a mathematical equation to say make 80 equal 100 that means 60 equals 75 etc.

The internet now has a number of customer review-driven sites – the biggest being Trip Advisor. I treat such sites with caution, because the primary reason many so-called reviews first get on them are as revenge for a bad meal, or a perceived sleight. And now there are legions working on 'reputational management' which means writing reviews for establishment on places like Trip Advisor.

My own maxims when using T A are: "all good" means it is fluff, "all bad" probably means it is bad ... but if there are a couple of "bad" among many "good" I will consider that the 'ayes' have it.

For those writing a review, it is not a bad idea to see what is said on the net. If it is contrary to your impression, think about it: have you got it wrong? Then sit down and write exactly what you thought after the restaurant visit. Firstly it is your review and your impression of what you found when you visited – and you must be true to yourself. Secondly there is lots balderdash on the internet.

You may also be writing to put your review on Trip Advisor or another site. Fair enough; it is not a bad way to get read. But still the same rules apply: the reader wants to know the whole story, not just that the food was great, or awful. How about the atmosphere, the service, the wine, the bread, the owner?

You are a restaurant reviewer and your readers will love you if when they go to a place, they agree with you. That is what makes you great: keeping your readers informed and amused.

Now go and do it.

8. Resources and links

www.howtowritebetter.net	Suzan St Maur's invaluable guide for aspiring writers as well as good tips for experienced scribes.
www.epicurious.com	A wealth of foody information - learn your way round this site and it will provide an invaluable tool.
Google.maps.co.uk	A great means to find wherever you want in the world. Tip use country suffix (co.uk, .fr. com.ph) to go to that country direct. However you can search address to get a location world wide.
Wikipedia	Love it or hate wiki they always provide and answer – not always right but not often wrong either.
www.winespectator.com/	Great site with all you are likely to need to know about wine – snag you have to subscribe.

Made in the USA
Lexington, KY
01 December 2017